Creating Communities of Good News

A Handbook for Small Group Facilitators

Mary LaCourse Mauren

Creating Communities of Good News

A Handbook for Small Group Facilitators

Mary LaCourse Mauren

Sheed & Ward

Sheed & Ward™ is a service of The National Catholic Reporter Publishing Company.

Library of Congress Catalog Card Number: 92-64035

ISBN: 1-55612-473-2

Published by: Sheed & Ward
115 E. Armour Blvd.
P.O. Box 419492
Kansas City, MO 64141-6492

To order, call: (800) 333-7373

Contents

1.

Catching a Vision of Facilitating Small Groups as Ministry

Focus: ministry that models/enables community building

Means: using a plant analogy to illustrate group growth

The ministry of facilitating begins with a desire to help create communities that are "good news." A facilitator basically enables the group to become a safe place for pilgrims to learn, grow, and journey with each other.

Jesus modeled shared leadership that is cooperative not competitive, and mutuality based (not stratified into inferior and superior). A good facilitator remembers that his/her main objective of community building is a ministry, a calling to help bring about the reign of God. This is best done as a team. There are a number of ways to form a team. If the group number is less than 15, and only one person is facilitating then he/she needs to find team support from the parish staff or adult education committee, for example. In addition, it is advisable to invite and disciple another member of the small group to be an assistant who becomes a main source of prayer, emotional support and consistent, reliable feedback (Chapter 9).

When the group is larger than 15, it is best to have one facilitator for every group of 8-10. Then all the facilitators form a team by meeting together regularly to share their lives and wisdom, pray and support each other.

Below is a simple horticultural analogy for the facilitator's ministry of creating communities. To help your small group get from this stage . . .

to THIS stage

1. **Prepare the Soil:** Keep the vision of community building in your mind and heart. Commitment to this ideal creates the "rich soil" of an empowered/empowering mindset. The focus helps the group become a safe and nurturing place for mutually journeying pilgrims.

2. **Choose the Appropriate Container:** Create the right setting to meet the particular needs of your specific group (known from needs assessment plus consideration of resources and facilities). The format needs to fit the group (Chapter 4). The right format, facilities, leadership and timing is important for forming and holding a group together. If you want to provide a support group for widowed "Seniors" for instance, the facilities need to be especially warm and accessible, daytime is best, a compassionate, older facilitator with grief awareness is a must, guided life/faith sharing is the best focus.

3. **Plant the Seeds:** Choose not only the appropriate setting but also the appropriate content and process that has the best chance of helping the group achieve its purpose. This is like planting the specific kind of seeds that will naturally produce that specific type of vegetation or flower. To produce a garden full of biblical spirituality for instance, it is vital to choose a Scripture study that uses the historical-contextual approach for scripture interpretation in the program materials, small group sharing that includes personal application/prayer and a trained facilitator committed to interdependent learning.

4. **Count on Sun:** No matter how well chosen the setting, content and process, the vital ingredient for a community experience is the warmth and caring modeled by the team members and "caught" by the group members. Facilitators warm the group with caring by putting relationships before function, creating a warm and safe climate (Chapters 4 and 5) and consistently integrating ways to get to know each other better (Chapter 6). A good facilitator takes such time to build bridges of trust and respect strong enough to undergird lively discussion and conflict management (using good communications skills [Chapter 3] and effective discussion leader techniques [Chapter 7]).

5. **Add Moisture:** Do everything you know how to do (capture a vision, carefully choose your setting, materials

and process, model and enable care-fullness), and at the same time, keep aware of creature limits and turn to God in faithful trust. Do this in your personal prayer life. Build such simple God consciousness into your ministry team meetings. This model of fidelity and humble neediness of Spirit power is contagious. Participants "catch" such prayerfulness and are thus set free to pray with and for each other as the facilitator enables various prayerways in the small group (Chapter 8). The moisture of prayerfulness is essential for quenching the thirst of a pilgrim people so often in the desert on their way to wholeness.

6. **Give It Time:** Trust in the process! It takes time to share and own a common vision, to form a ministry team, to research needs, to choose appropriate setting and content, to grow in ease of communication and prayerfulness, to build bridges of trust, respect and caring. There is no microwave method of formation. No one expects an overnight harvest from any garden. Rather, trust in the dynamic of group process. Learn the stages of group development and the styles of leadership that energize each stage (Chapter 2). Trust in good communication skills (Chapter 3) and discussion leader techniques that create safety and mutuality within the group (Chapter 7). Make a commitment to the time, energy, method and people that will equip you with the awareness and skills necessary for personal leadership growth. This is a long-term investment in bringing about the reign of God.

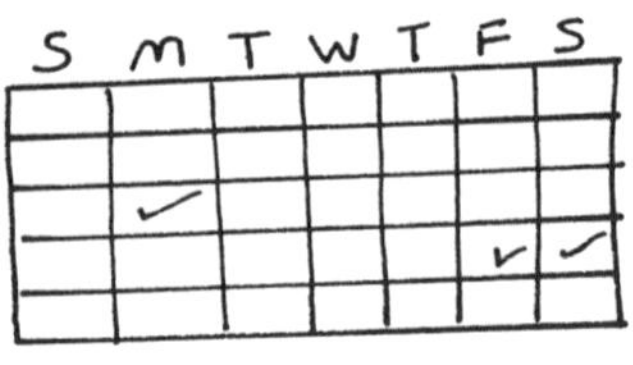

7. **Expect to Cultivate:** The best way to keep your community garden hoed and weed-free is to build in regular evaluation. Keep aware of what is working in a group and what is not by using any of several verbal or nonverbal methods of evaluation (Chapter 9). Such processes provide constructive information via affirmation and suggestions for improvement, thus motivating for change in nonthreatening ways. In addition to assessing strengths and weaknesses of a program, the process of feedback helps develop honest and real interpersonal relationships. Facilitators who choose and disciple an assistant into the process of feedback will discover a simple, effective way to keep the group healthy and growing.

8. **Enjoy the Harvest:** Celebrate peoplemaking whenever and wherever it happens throughout the lifetime of any small group but most especially when a group adjourns. Building in closure time is vital. It is a way of affirming individual gifts and acknowledging the gift of journeying together as well as setting people free to continue growing another time with another group. Plan then to celebrate with potlucks, parties, rituals, liturgy, prayer, drama and song fests whenever it works. It is always time to enjoy and celebrate life as it is happening as well as to bring special closure to a significant community experience (Chapter 10).

2.

Knowing/Staying Mindful of Group Dynamics

Focus: understanding group purpose/stages of development/needs

Means: information about how groups grow, what groups need

Naivete' about the ways groups begin, grow and mature causes many groups to die on the vine, their potential flowering arrested by ignorance. If however, facilitators of groups are aware and stay mindful of the dynamics of group purpose, development and related leadership needs, they can effectively channel their energy toward achieving a common goal. When groups experience satisfying and mutually gratifying achievements AND relationships it is evidence of time and energy well spent together. Aware and skillful facilitators can cultivate this.

Definition of Group Dynamics

A group is a collection of people in interdependent relationships who have a common bond and/or purpose.

Group dynamics refers to the impelling motivation, interaction and process that pulls a group together, helps them continue to be and work together toward a common goal.

Purpose of Every Group

There are two purposes or concerns of every group. One is to accomplish the work of the group (TASK). The other is to care for the people in the group (RELATIONSHIP).

In the long run, both of these concerns (concern for the task to be done and concern for the relationships between group members) need attention if the group is to stay alive.

It is helpful to remember that ALL the group members and not just the facilitator (who is also a group member) share responsibility for the task and relationship functions of the group. In the beginning of a new group, the facilitator may perform most of these functions. By offering consistent affirmation to other group members who give their gift, others pick up their share of the responsibility for making the group work. Below are some examples of group member functions that help get the task done and take care of the group members.

A. **Task functions:**

Work together to get the task done

1. initiating: attempting to get the task started via defining terms, suggestions/ideas/ways to move ahead.
2. informing: giving or receiving information, opinions, facts, or suggestions without being asked.
3. structuring: attempting to keep on track and keep on time
4. building: clarifying/elaborating on the thoughts of others

5. summarizing: pulling ideas together in a digested form and restating them as a way of keeping the meeting moving
6. evaluating: critiquing and testing the group for consensus on suggestions and conclusions. The aim is agreement.

B. **Relationship functions:**

Care about/for each other

1. offering norms: suggesting group rules or better ways of relating and/or working together
2. gatekeeping: inviting participation into the discussion.
3. climate-making: enabling a freedom to enter into the group process by sharing one's own thoughts/ feelings freely; expressing feelings sensed in the group; listening with understanding; respectfully responding to all contributions; encouraging minority opinion; offering appropriate tension relief.
4. harmonizing: attempting to reconcile disagreements or differences; exploring compromise with others; soothing.
5. compromising: changing positions; modifying ideas or trying on a new idea for the sake of the group

Surround Each Task with Heart to Grow a Healthy Group

Stages of Group Development

Every group goes through developmental stages. It is helpful to remember that every time a new member enters a group the whole group development process returns to stage one. The leader must then guide the group once more through the tasks of stage one of group development (beginning with welcoming, introductions, historicizing).

A. Stage One: Forming . . . the tactful stage

member's concern: "Will I be included?"; "Is it safe here?"

facilitator's concern: "How can I help bring about an atmosphere in which everyone feels safe enough to share or to remain silent?"

task: create a climate of physical/psychological comfort, an island of safety.

means: arrange comfortable setting; offer friendly greetings at the door; begin with self-introduction by all group members; help identify and acknowledge anxieties; assist in clarifying/sharing expectations; establishing ground rules such as "individual differences are to be respected; confidentiality is expected."

leadership: a creative style that is both directive and welcoming; ability to motivate and involve participants.

B. Stage Two: Informing . . . the factful Stage

member's concern: "What are we here for?"

facilitator's concern: Initially, "How much history and vision will enable this group to productively discuss our purpose (what we hope to achieve together) and manner (the way in which it will be done)?"; later, "Is the group doing what it has agreed to do?"

task: to achieve clarification and ownership of/commitment to a common goal.

means: offer (or elicit from old group members) the appropriate amount of history and vision that will bring new group members on board and equip them with information; facilitate a group centered discussion that clarifies what the group hopes to achieve together; summarize group purpose and discuss how the group wants to achieve its defined purpose; keep the goal and objectives before the group; appropriately challenge the group to take action that will move it toward its purpose; build in evaluation as a means of accountability to the agreed upon purpose.

leadership: flexible directive style that organizes well; helps establish procedures to decide and be accountable in order to achieve the established group purpose/task

C. Stage Three: Storming . . . the power-full stage

member's concern: "Who is in charge here? How much influence may I have in the life of the group?"

facilitator's concern: "How can I help surface and affirm individual gifts so that we all share (and not compete) in the leadership responsibility for this group"; "How can I best handle the conflicts that arise?"

task: to provide a safe climate for expressing differing opinions, sharing different gifts; to help conflicts be recognized, diagnosed, defused and (if possible) honestly reconciled.

means: active listening—especially paraphrasing; using conflict resolution skills.

leadership: a delegative style that entrusts and empowers others to share in the life/direction of the group.

D. Stage Four: Re-Forming . . . the care-full stage

member's concern: "What is my responsibility on this team?"

facilitator's concern: "How can I help elicit and communicate trust in each member's contributions?"

task: focus on team building.

means: group exercises, systems and procedures aimed at team building; encouragement and positive feedback.

leadership: a coordinative style that care-fully appropriates/utilizes materials and personal efforts toward the overall purpose of the group.

E. Stage Five: Performing . . . the fruit-full stage

member's concern: "How can I help maintain honest and real relationships in my responsibilities here?"

facilitator's concern: "How can I best support the interpersonal relationships in this group?"; "How do I best affirm the spirit and productivity in our group?"

task: team support and communal problem solving

means: educational efforts toward team building; honest interaction between interdependent members; reminding them that all groups move to closure as some or eventually all members *move on* or the purpose of the group is accomplished.

leadership: a collaborative style that consults/solves problems together

Group Leadership

The role of leadership in Christian community is extremely important during this time of crucial transition in Church. To be effective, the Christian leader keeps in mind that he/she is called to be both model of gospel values and skilled facilitator of human resources in serving a particular Christian community.

There are many leadership styles depending on a person's background, self concept and awareness of group need. Ideally, the leader uses all four styles of leadership as they are appropriate. Note that as a group matures, the effective leader transfers more and more of the responsibility for group growth to the group members.

The four basic styles each include some proportion of relationship and task:

1. high relationship and low task style (works well for a group with mostly a social or support focus)

2. high task and low relationship style (works well for a group with a short term commitment with a lot of work to do)
3. high task and high relationship style (works well for a new group)
4. low task and low relationship style (works well for a mature group)

Whatever style of leadership you are most comfortable with, remember there are a few basic functions to keep in mind and follow sequentially:

1. create a climate of warmth and safety
2. encourage interaction between members
3. keep to the agreed upon task
4. direct the group toward its purpose
5. intervene when the dynamics prevent progress
6. evaluate group progress regularly

In *Collaborative Ministry* by Loughlan Sofield and Carroll Juliano, the authors suggest using the above in a "Rolodex method." They suggest mentally (or actually) printing on five cards these absolutely basic functions for group leadership, focusing on one at a time and following them sequentially.

A last note to consider is to provide for a warm, appropriate closure process when the group dynamic or time or task commitment indicates it (see Chapter 10).

Suggested Resource

Joining Together by David W. Johnson and Frank P. Johnson.

The Last Word

Watch for *symbiosis* to happen as group members grow together in unity. This is when the whole adds up to more than the sum of its parts.

3.

Remembering to Use Good Communication Skills

Focus: maximizing chances of hearing/being heard

Means: information and exercises for hearing and speaking accurately

Definition

Communication is more than the expression of thoughts and feelings, it is also the revelation of one's own reality. Effective communicating begins with an open, honest, caring attitude that invites a verbal and nonverbal interchange of feelings, thoughts, information and self disclosure. Good communicating is a style of talking and behaving that sustains relationships. This includes a sense of feeling comfortable with oneself and one's feelings, an ability to listen attentively with genuine caring, a freedom and skill to verbalize thoughts, feelings and needs accurately and appropriately; and knowing how to cope with criticism, manage conflicts and say "No" when appropriate.

Blessings

Some blessings of effective communicating include: knowing you have maximized your chances of being heard and of hearing the other; the privilege of experiencing being in the heart of another and tucking the other in your own heart; getting your needs met in an honest, assertive, caring way; sharing in the life giving energy of mutual relationships; the high efficiency functioning of a team who work together out of the flow of right relationships (rather than in spite of nonworking relationships).

Elements

Some elements of good communication include: visual elements (eye contact, distance, facial expression, gestures and posture, body orientation); verbal elements (loudness, rate of speech, fluency, affect); and verbal elements (use of complete sentences, ability to focus, qualifying statements).

Process

In the process of communicating there are two focuses: 1) the encoder who formulates and sends the message and 2) the decoder who receives and interprets the message. Real dialogue happens when sender and receiver both are open and honestly aware of their individual barriers and are committed to practice good communication skills.

Barriers

There are real barriers to communicating well. Poor self image, language associations, prejudices, fears and defenses, anxieties, and behavior patterns that are unassertive, aggressive or passive-aggressive will get in the way of sending and receiving clear, straight messages. These hindrances act as a selective filter system which admits some parts of the message, rejects some parts and twists others. Each barrier is an obstacle that stops, distorts or sidetracks healthy communication.

Overcoming Barriers

There are ways of overcoming barriers to good communication. The way to begin is always to look at your own self in a process of reflection. Reflection has to do with listening to yourself. It is not dwelling on a problem in a way that only rehashes symptoms. Reflection has to do with taking time to be quiet in order to relax, focus yourself, think about the situation in a way that asks, "Why is this happening?" AND THEN to listen to your feelings and insights respond.

God created human beings to live in wholeness (a state of harmony within our being, with other human beings and with the cosmos). If we pay attention to a sense of imbalance in any of these areas of life, we can take better care of ourselves. Our body can signal us about an imbalance with headaches, hypertension, hyperalertness, compulsive behavior, restlessness, a kind of being *out of touch* or possibly a sense of being on an emotional roller coaster. Feelings, or the movement of energy (up or down) that accompanies any stress, are probably the best alert system for our need to restore harmony. Our feelings communicate that there is an imbalance somewhere needing attention and caring. The first step in overcoming obstacles to good communication then is to take care of the communicator by getting in touch with feelings and caring for needs.

The following experiences will demonstrate one method to help surface feelings and needs.

Exercise. Pick a problem situation. Find a time/place to be quiet. Relax and focus into the quiet within. Ask yourself the following questions:

1. How do I feel? (angry? afraid? sad? happy? anxious? hurt? peaceful? pleased? annoyed? intimidated? guilty? uncomfortable?). Finish the sentence, "I feel ________________ because ______________________."
2. What do I need? According to Maslow's research, all people have the same basic needs, each depending on the previous one in hierarchical manner. These are: physiological needs; safety needs; acceptance needs; esteem needs; self-actualization needs; self transcendence needs. Some might describe all individual needs as fitting under the umbrella of the basic right of self-integrity and the basic right of self-determination. Finish the sentence, "I need ________________ because ______________________."
3. What could I do? First, ask God to grace you with a clean heart and right spirit. Be open then to the same

Spirit that created you. Believe that you will have wisdom to meet your needs. Then, brainstorm possible solutions in your mind, generating as many ideas as possible BEFORE evaluating. Then choose the best alternative (stated in the form of a specific, detailed, behavioral objective that is manageable/measurable).

Finish ten sentences beginning with, "What might work is ________________."

Later, finish this sentence. "I will ____________________."

The first step will be ____________________________.

Guidelines for Effective Communicating

Know that attitude determines behavior. Every person who wants to follow Jesus must enter the world of relationships as he did. Scripture shows and tells us that Jesus' basic guideline in living out his relationships was the law of love. Love of God, love of neighbor as self. It is helpful then to give yourself a *love check* regarding your style of communicating. Do you have a clean heart, right spirit, love intentioned, open attitude within? If the heart is right and you have a teachable attitude, learning how to communicate in a loving way is comparatively easy. If you consider communication skills to be the tools for loving, interpersonal bridge-building, they will be worth any amount of time, energy, and personal struggle to acquire. If, on the other hand, you are not convinced of the value of communication skills, you will resist learning these skills instead of persevering as an open, willing student. Remember, resistance always has meaning, so ask yourself, "What am I afraid of?" if you feel resistant.

Understand that feelings are neutral—neither right nor wrong. Feelings are *energy in motion*. They are chemical reactions activated by the autonomic nervous system. These chemical reactions are caused by the brain responding to a stimulus that is perceived and interpreted. The chain of reaction goes like this: 1) Stress stimulus—2) Thought (perception and interpretation according to old tapes)—3) Glands secrete into vascular system—4) Physiological response (heart beats faster, face reddens, sweating, etc. to prepare the body to meet a need or overcome an obstacle to what is needed)—5) Action follows, aimed at meeting the perceived need—6) A state of balance follows right action. It is essential then for good health to get in touch with our feelings—to acknowledge, validate and honor them as true signals of need. Begin to increase and use your feeling vocabulary because all dimensions of human communication are influenced by our feelings. Naming and claiming feelings then is central to effective communication.

Avoid red flag words. They create distance and defensiveness. Words like *people*, *everyone*, *no-one*, are such generalizations that their use makes the discussion seem remote from the here and now. The expressions, *always* and *never* cause distrust of the speaker because experience tells us that life is not lived in terms of such dogmatic absolutes. Statements including these two words do not ring true. Another group of red flag words fall under the heading of judgmental. These words tend to tyrannize with condemnation in one degree or another: should, ought, cannot, fault, blame. These words feel like an attack to the listener (even when spoken to yourself). Confrontational phrases tend to be conversation stoppers because they contribute to the listener feeling attacked or defensive. These defense-building phrases include: You are. . . . Why do/don't you. . . . How can/could you. . . . How come you. . . . Challenge yourself to tune into the use of red flag words and the affect on you as speaker and as listener. Then choose to eliminate such words one at a time. Ask one close friend to support you towards this goal.

Honor both left brain and right brain styles of thinking. Research today tells us that left brain style of thinking is sequential, verbal, analytical, rational, objective and detail-focused. Right brain style of thinking is simultaneous, visual, synthetical, intuitive, subjective and overview-focused. Our basic need is to be *wholebrained*, encouraging and respecting what each side of the brain can do. Imagination and logic need to work together in cooperation and confidence for the common good. In ourselves and others, we need to honor the different ways that we and other people work things out, even when using *unconventional* approaches to studying and problem-solving.

Skills for Communicating Well

Learn to listen attentively and with caring in nonverbal and verbal ways. With or without words, good listening begins with an attitude of respect, of treating each other with regard, of letting others matter in our lives. Each of us can pretend to listen or can hear another's words but be passively uninvolved. Listening is hard work at times, particularly when you do not agree with the one speaking. Remember however that listening well does not necessarily mean agreeing with the other's statements. It does mean attending to the speaker with focused awareness, honest expectation and an intention to understand the other's feelings and thoughts.

1. Next to attitude checks, our nonverbal ways of listening are the most important way to communicate "I am with you." Psychologists call this attending, the most important skill of active listening. Attending includes the way we use facial expression and eye behavior, body movement, gesture and touch, and use of personal space to communicate real presence to another. Ask yourself if your whole face and use of body communicates what is in your heart. Then consider giving the Spirit permission to make you aware of either an attitude barrier or nonverbal obstacle to offering the ministry of listening to those who need it.

2. In addition to nonverbal listening skills, there are verbal listening helpers. These include asking clarifying questions that bring vague material into sharper focus by responding to the speaker in terms of admitting one's own confusion, thereby avoiding the implications of criticism. "I'm confused. Could you say it another way? I'm trying to understand." are verbal statements of listening. Paraphrasing, an active listening skill, is a process of reflecting back the other's message in fewer words. Offering a concise summary without added perceptions, judgements or advice tests your understanding

and implicitly invites the speaker to clear up confusion. Perception checking is another verbal listening skill that goes beyond the summarizing focus of paraphrasing. It is a key method of clearing up confusion and correcting misperceptions before they become misunderstandings. First paraphrase what you think you hear ("You expressed some doubt."). Next, ask for confirmation directly about the accuracy of your perception ("Did I understand you correctly?").

3. The way to check your verbal listening skills is to ask yourself after asking clarifying questions, perception checking or paraphrasing, "Did I really WANT to understand, trust and relate to the other or was I more interested in blaming or defending?" If appropriate, also ask the speaker, "Do you sense that I understood you?" The ministry of listening offers others the gift of being understood, cared about and cared for.

Learn to speak the truth directly. Take responsibility for your own thoughts and feelings by using "I" language. Sending "I" messages allows each person to OWN their own feelings/thoughts/needs/problems. I need to acknowledge that it is MY problem whenever my needs go unmet, when I am dissatisfied/troubled. I need verbal clarity that begins with self knowledge and is expressed with clear, "I think/I feel/I need" statements instead of vagueness, hesitant hinting, crazy-making double messages or disguising my need with cover up plurals such as, "We should" or "Let's all." Distinguishing characteristics of sending a healthy "I" message is that it is personal, honest, specific, noncondemning and congruent with inner beliefs and real feelings.

Practice the "I" message by correcting the following sentences so they each clearly expresses where the speaker is at:

1. Things are going better within our group.
2. Most of us agree that something needs to change here.
3. We should begin and end each gathering of Christians with prayer.
4. Everyone knows that feelings get in the way of efficiency.

5. No one should ever be afraid of sharing in this group.
6. Someone should tell the speaker to talk louder.
7. You are always so quiet.
8. Let's all make a commitment to be here on time from now on.
9. You should really learn to relax more.

Learn How to Cope With Criticism, Manage Conflicts And Say "No"

Criticism, according to the dictionary is the act of analyzing and judging the quality of something. In human experience criticism usually means *finding fault* with a person. *Fault, blame, should, ought* are the judgmental words that express a critical attitude. There are emotional consequences of not responding in an assertive way. "Our stomach's keep score," one armchair philosopher once said. The *scorekeeping* refers to memories of past experience connected to censure, blame, and severe judgment. Even when someone says, "I'd like to give you some constructive criticism," the word *constructive* does nothing to alleviate fear. Understanding previous associations with the experience of criticism increases awareness of emotional hangovers that get in the way of responding assertively. Three ineffective responses when faced with criticism are either withdrawal, justification or counterattack. Sometimes such a reaction is due to the fact that the criticism strikes too close to home and everyone wants to save face. Even when the criticism is a truth delivered "for your own good," the wrapping of judgment makes it most difficult to respond in a positive way and unwrap that truth. It is possible to cope with criticism in a way that allows the listener to learn more about themselves, become less defensive and disarm the critic at the same time. Here are some suggestions.

1. Seek more information when criticized. Ask or guess about specifics of a complaint in order to clarify. Paraphrasing the speaker's ideas usually defuses the emotional intensity because the speaker feels heard. Asking about the consequences of your behavior on the other

will help both to see what unmet needs caused the reaction.

2. Agree with the speaker regarding whatever truth is spoken. Nondefensive responses that accept responsibility for one's own words/behavior that affected another calms both down. If it's impossible to agree personally, agree in principle about how aggravating certain behaviors are. At the very least, agree with the critic's perception. Other persons have a right to perceive things their way without you having to accept responsibility.

Managing conflict begins with an understanding of or definition of conflict. Conflict is simply any situation in which apparently incompatible needs surface at the same time. Since it is not possible to have a relationship in which both parties always have compatible needs, the first thing to understand about conflict is that it is inevitable. It is unwise therefore to spend energy trying to avoid it. Ignoring conflict does not work either. Feelings not attended to simply go underground and get displaced against an innocent party or time-bomb a later encounter. To love one another means honoring relationships and that means dealing with conflict to the best of our ability. If those involved, however, are psychologically unhealthy to the point that they cannot participate in productive dialogue and/or are chemically dependent, conflict is unresolvable. Here are some effective ways to try to manage conflict:

1. Reflect, analyzing and diagnosing the source of the problem. Search your own heart regarding feelings. Let them lead you to your needs. Ask yourself "What is my need in this situation that seems incompatible with the other person's need?" Use 'I' language to clarify it. "I feel . . . because . . . ." "I need . . . ."

2. Create a safe environment: choose as ideal a time/place as possible; aim your heart at reconciliation; initiate the dialogue. Remember to own the problem using "I" language: "I have a problem . . . , when you . . . (offensive behavior), then . . . (effect on me). I feel. . . ."

3. Express your need to be heard accurately: "Do you understand what I am trying to say?" or "What do you

think I am trying to communicate?" Repeat your need to be understood until you feel heard.

4. Make your request directly and honestly—no hints/demands: I need. . . . Rather, say, "I want or I need . . . ." "I request . . . ."
5. Listen to the other person's perspective in order to learn their needs. Use active listening to understand where the other is at: How do you feel? What do you need?
6. Enable a problem solving negotiation session: restate both sets of needs; mutually define the problem; brainstorm possible solutions (no evaluating yet); choose 2-3 alternatives that might work; discuss pros/cons of each; choose one; set up checkup meeting to evaluate progress.

Setting Goals For Improving Communication Skills

Identify your communication problem by completing the following:

1. When communicating with _________ (parents, siblings, spouse, children, friends, co-workers, authority figures), I find it hard to _____ because _____ .
2. I am uncomfortable communicating:
   a. in these particular situations ____________________
   b. on these particular topics ______________________
   c. in this particular setting _______________________
3. Define your problem behaviorally: (who is involved; what are the typical circumstances; what is the specific offensive behavior): When ______________ happens (what) with ____________________ (who), I find it hard to ________________ .
4. Establish a behavioral goal that is complete and specific, measurable and manageable, includes the people involved in a target situation and the circumstances in which it occurs. Describe in detail how you want to behave in that circumstance: "The next time I am criti-

cized by ___________, first I want to choose a non-defensive attitude. Then I want to verbally agree with whatever truth honestly applies to me, or if it doesn't feel like truth, I want to agree with my critic's right to his/her own perceptions. I will use 'I' statements to communicate this."

5. Give yourself permission to be a learner, to take time to grow into your new behavior. Try writing down both sides of the dialogue in an imagined scene. Rehearse your new behavior through visualization. Practice or role play your target behavior with someone safe and solicit their feedback before trying the new skill with your target person.

6. To keep your comfort level high and your anxiety level low, break down your goal into small, easily attainable steps. Then proceed one step at a time toward acquiring then integrating assertive communication skills

Suggested Resource

Words Made Flesh by Fran Ferder

The Last Word

The steps to maturity are necessarily immature. Take that first step that will give you the ability to communicate a full range of thoughts and emotions with confidence and skill.

4.

Creating the Climate

Focus: providing a safe, warm space for group gathering and interaction that expresses hospitality

Means: preparing the environment via careful planning of the physical setting and care-full attitudes

The Need For Hospitality

One of the most basic ways to begin creating Christian community is to focus on hospitality as expressed in warm and welcoming attitudes, words and behavior. This is never more important than when a group first gathers.

There are many ways to create a welcoming environment in which group members can grow to feel like they "belong." This "at home" experience comes from attention to the physical and psychological comfort and safety of the participants.

It is important then to have a welcoming attitude, to learn and integrate the words and behavior of hospitality. The initial step is to prepare an inviting and workable environment. Do this with careful attention to the practical logistics of choosing the building, room, seating arrangement, temperature, air circulation, lighting and equipment that will work best for your people and purposes.

It is not only the physical environment that creates a comfortable climate, it is also the facilitator's care-full attitudes, words and behavior. This includes the leader's assumptions about Christianity, ministry and leadership (and particularly facilitating) as well as awareness of and commitment to adult education principles. It may be necessary to reflect on and clarify a familiar idea, to change some mistaken beliefs and to integrate some new concepts. This open and willing attitude toward growth will help the facilitator grow to BE a welcoming person. It is such a presence that best creates an island of safety where people can feel free to be themselves, where each is free to share or remain silent.

The Call to Hospitality

Jesus IS Good News! This means that the reign of God, the fullness of God present was expressed in Jesus. He is the model for a life and ministry that welcomes and invites participation in community. This free and freeing manner of eliciting committed response from a group does not come just from practicing the best techniques. Rather, it comes from personal commitment to a wholistic spirituality, one that integrates physical, mental and spiritual balance. A person who is openly committed to healthy holiness is attractive, a welcome sign for tired seekers (just as Jesus was). This is the best way to invite and welcome folks into communities of Good News.

The best news is that Jesus was faithful to becoming all he was created to be. First of all, he responded to his call and was disciple to God with an attitude of surrender and trust. He could thus receive love, acceptance and empowerment from God. And Jesus loved himself with a holy self love. He was free to be himself. Jesus shared that wholeness in a ministry to others that was free and freeing, challenging and accepting, healing and reconciling, powerful and empowering. His personal growth was lived out in the company of God's people, with a small community for support.

The basic quality needed to minister out of Jesus' vision is to integrate his attitude of committed openness. It is imperative then to begin with willingness to answer the call to relationship, to discipleship that is transformative. Then staying within the large faith family but with a small community for support we can grow in awareness, healing and wholeness in all relationships; that is, in trusting surrender to God, in a holy love of self and in honest, caring and mutuality based relationships with others.

The Practice of Hospitality

Create a comfortable physical environment, being careful about the setting.

1. decide on the building and room that best facilitates the group comfort and purpose (a home living room for a grief support group, the parish rectory for the liturgy committee)

2. arrange the seating that best facilitates the group process (straight lines of metal chairs in lecture hall style hardly ever works; make curved semi circles if the group is large; pull chairs in tight and "knock knees" if there are many small groups close together in a room; eliminate empty chairs in small group settings)

3. check that the temperature is comfortable for the age and activity level of the group (anticipate that large groups with high activity warm up a room quickly; conversely, smaller, more sedentary groups need a higher temperature; best to check with the group after about 30 minutes regarding comfort level)

4. ventilation for adequate air circulation is vital (air room out before group meets; check that no one is sitting in a draft; ask group to help take responsibility for comfort level)

5. see that the lighting is suitable for the function of the group (if reading and paper work is a prime function, give stronger lighting; if the group is a small support group, soft lighting is adequate)

6. be sure that the equipment and materials needed are on hand and in good working condition (overhead projector has an extra light bulb, tape recorder has an extension cord, handouts are readable and in order)

7. consider having a focal point such as an open bible on a stand, an inspirational poster, a cluster of different sized votive lights, flowers

Create a safe psychological environment. Be even more carefull about clearly establishing the basic underlying principles for creating a warm and safe environment. This includes:

understanding ministry as gifts responding to call; understanding leadership as empowerment; understanding facilitating as enabling a safe, warm place where community can happen; and a commitment to integrate the principles of adult education into any format used.

1. Though it is helpful to remember that call to ministry comes first from baptism, it is even more helpful to remember that call to a particular ministry is related to natural and developed gifts. It is true that "grace builds on nature." It is important then to know and accept one's gifts and minister from them in order to prevent burnout. God doesn't ask a highly introverted and analytical scientist, for example, to facilitate a youth group.

   It is important to realize that it is not necessary to respond to every need or request for help. God is the prime ecologist of time and energy and will not ask us to be or do more than we can. So when we minister out of call rather than compulsive caretaking or spiritual workaholism, we can count on God providing enough time, energy and wisdom as we cooperate.

2. It is vital to examine your beliefs about leadership. The best vision of leadership is that enfleshed by Jesus—that of empowering others to feel more lovable and capable (the two most basic human needs).

   Leading a group has nothing to do with power as control and authority. Rather, leaders need to think of power as effectiveness. Leadership then is about helping others "to be able"/effective, to be empowered! Of course, what we give away in service comes more from who we are than what we do. It is imperative then to be committed to personal growth towards wholeness, a spirituality that integrates physical, mental, spiritual balance and integrity. Our basic prayer as leaders might be, "Create in me a clean heart, O Lord and renew a right spirit within me." or "Renew the world, dear God, and begin with me."

   Below is a basic checklist for good leaders:

- has a listening attitude that seeks to understand not to blame and defend
- has awareness of his/her own limitations and is free to ask for help
- can intervene assertively when the group needs it
- has a cooperative not a competitive spirit and so is able to work in a shared leadership model
- is flexible and able to adapt, not rigid and threatened by change/spontaneity

These attitudes and skills needed for effective christian leadership are what this book is about.

3. Reflect on your understanding of facilitating. It is important to understand facilitating as enabling a group to both relate and function well together. The facilitator is not teacher, counselor, expert or guru. A facilitator is a skilled minister who empowers a group to feel more lovable and capable individually and communally. This is done by creating a climate of safety in which the assigned task is done efficiently (using good discussion leader techniques that encourage interaction among the members, keeping on track and on time, intervening when group purpose is not being accomplished, building in evaluation). This is also done by being attentive to relationships, by putting people before task, relationship before function, care before efficiency.

4. Be aware and committed to sound principles of adult education. Ideal conditions for adult learning include freedom of expression, mutual trust and respect, shared responsibility, physical and emotional comfort, and an atmosphere of hospitality. It is vital then to be aware and committed to sound principles of adult education. Remember that adults:

   a. learn best when they can choose from a variety of learning activities, styles, topics

   b. respond to programs they've helped plan

   c. participate when their needs/interests are treated as important

d. respond best when physically/emotionally comfortable
e. need an atmosphere of mutual freedom of expression
f. need to be self-directing in their learning
g. are resources as well as learners in an interdependent learning atmosphere
h. learn best when their learning situation is related to the needs of their stage of life
i. need to evaluate themselves/program

Suggested Resource

The Minister of God by Helen Doohan, Ph.D

The Last Word

The silent question of each new group member is, "Is this a safe place to be?" The facilitator's basic question needs to be, "How can I best help to create a warm and safe environment for this group?"

5.

Using Openings/Breaks That Create Ease

Focus: beginning group time/providing creative breaks in ways that are meaningful, create comfort, energize

Means: employing appropriate words, music, stories, prayer or exercises as openings/transitions

This book began by visioning good facilitating as the ministry of community building. Then we looked at the importance both of understanding how groups work and of using good communication skills for healthy group development.

Besides visioning, awareness of group dynamics and using good communication skills, it is vital to learn the ways of creating a warm and safe environment. All of this is foundational for successful facilitating.

It is time now to turn to some specific facilitating SKILLS: creating helpful openings/breaks and getting-to-know-you processes; practicing effective discussion leader techniques; enabling prayer ways; using evaluating techniques and satisfying closure methods.

We begin with the basic skill of getting a group off to a good start with welcoming and meaningful words that create ease and give focus to the meeting. We will then look at taking creative breaks that both help a large group get acquainted and energize participants during long meetings.

Helpful Openings

Introduce group time in ways that welcome and include:

1. Begin with words as simple as "I'd like to welcome you to. . . ." or "Welcome to an evening of. . . ." or "Welcome to St. ______________ . My name is ____________________ ." Consider adding "Please turn to the ones on either side of you and introduce yourself." Affirm attendees for spending the time and energy to be there.

2. Be sure to attend to *housekeeping* details early: Locate bathrooms and telephones; announce times of breaks.

3. Here are some introductions that include everyone:

   a. For an established group that has guests, ask anyone who has brought a guest to introduce them. Lead a response of applause or welcome each in the name of the group.

   b. For a large gathering of people from all over the city, (diocese, state or nation), welcome by identifying the parishes (or cities/regions/states) people come from. Ask them to stand or raise their hands and be acknowledged in some way.

   c. For a large gathering of ministerial people, welcome them by naming different ministries and having them identify themselves by standing or raising a hand.

   d. For the orientation meeting of a long established group that is welcoming new members, ask all to stand. Then ask the founding members of the group (or those who have been members the longest (name the years) to sit down. Go by 5 year increments (or whatever is appropriate). Ask each group of "veterans" to sit down in turn until the only ones standing are the brand new members. Welcome them with a round of applause and suggest they go to the "veterans" with specific questions about membership.

After introductions, use an appropriate means to help introduce the purpose of the gathering.

1. *Music* that reinforces the theme is a great way to begin if the facilitator is comfortable leading with voice, guitar or even tape recorded music. When the focus is a social justice discussion or a scripture course on the Prophets for instance, an appropriate song would be, "The Lord Hears the Cry of the Poor." For a Marriage Preparation, Marriage Enrichment evening, sing "Love One Another."

2. *Stories* often make a good opening because they capture people's attention quickly. A book such as *Song of the Bird* or *One Minute Wisdom,* by Anthony de Mello contains helpful anecdotes or stories such as the following (perfect for a small support group or evening focusing on Spirituality):

   > "To a disciple who was forever complaining about others the Master said, 'If it is peace you want, seek to change yourself, not other people. It is easier to protect your feet with slippers than to carpet the whole of the earth.'"
   > —(page 38, One Minute Wisdom)

   Sometimes getting in touch with part of one's own story is the most appropriate way to begin. For instance, ask each to reflect on the remote reasons for their attendance at that particular meeting. At a gathering of catechists for instance, ask each to remember someone who modeled holiness for them in their formative years. Parents at a Sacramental Preparation meeting might reflect on the way their parents communicated the importance of sacrament for them. If the meeting focuses on Ministry Formation, ask each to think of one time when they really EXPERIENCED ministry offered them. If the facilitator models by sharing his/her own mini story, others are set free to share their story. After a moment of reflection, suggest each silently attend to their grateful heart before moving on to the meeting's content.

3. *Prayer* is always appropriate in a Christian setting. It is particularly helpful to *read Scripture prayerfully* as a way to focus. (Consult Cruden's *Concordance* to find a

reading connected to the theme). Quieting one's spirit by Centering is also a good beginning for certain gatherings. (Consult *Sadhana* by Anthony de Mello for aids on centering prayer.) Either formal prayer together or a spontaneous prayer by the facilitator is also appropriate. (Consult Chapter 8 for other suggestions.)

4. Using appropriate quotes to begin the content part of the meeting might be very helpful. Consult *Bartlett's Quotations* for possibilities.

5. Some exercises would be valuable for bringing the evening's topic into focus. For example, instead of only silent reflection on one's story (as outlined in Story Openings above), suggest that groups of three or four share those faith stories. Then surface feelings and insights related to the evening's topic.

Creative Breaks

If the meeting is large and long enough to deserve break time, consider the following possibilities as ways to get acquainted with more people/re-energize the group. Direct them to always introduce themself as step one.

1. Concerning Birth Information

   a. *Birth order*. Ask all first borns (then last borns, then middle children) to stand. Gather them in different corners and find a partner. Take a break together and compare notes about their birth order experiences.

   b. *Birth month*. Ask everyone to get up and start walking around the room saying their birth month aloud until they find another to spend the break with. Suggest each share three interesting facts about themself with their break partner.

   c. *Birth place*. Indicate parameters of the USA in the room (indicate which corners represent Maine to Florida and where to locate the West coast from Washington to California). Indicate a separate place for Alaska, Hawaii and anyplace else other than continental USA. Ask each to locate themselves on the "room map." Choose at least one other with whom to spend the break time and compare reason for moving from or staying in birthplace.

d. *Birth date by decades.* Indicate the beginning of a timeline continuum beginning with the 20's or 30's through the 80's. Ask each to gather themselves according to their decade of birth and find one or two persons to join for break time. Share particular *wisdom* gained from this decade in life.

e. *Shortest or longest first name.* Indicate the place in the room where continuum of shortest to longest begins. Ask each to stand according to the length of name and find a nearby partner for break time. Share any interesting experience having to do with your name.

2. By Externals

a. Indicate the beginning of a color continuum of lightest to darkest. Ask each to stand according to hair or eye color (from lightest to darkest). Ask each to gather on the continuum as indicated and find a nearby partner for break time. Share any blessing/frustration connected with your coloring.

b. Ask each to walk around finding someone else who has the same color of shoes (or sweater/blouse, etc). Join that person for break time. Share three interesting facts about yourself with your partner.

3. By Preferences

a. *Type of music.* Ask each to think of their favorite kind of music (opera, symphonic or classical, country, jazz, rock and roll) then walk around the room stating their preference until they find someone who matches their preference. Take break time together sharing about your musical interest.

b. *Favorite season.* Ask each to think of their favorite season and why they chose it. Indicate which season matches the four corners of the room and ask participants to head for their "corner" to find a partner for break time. Share seasonal reflections.

c. *Kind of pet you had as a child (or have now).* Ask each person to think of that animal and the sound it makes. Have them walk around making that animal noise until they find another who's making the same sound. Suggest that those who have always been "petless" walk around with hands over their ears until finding another petless partner for break time. Share about your pets (or reasons for being "petless").

Suggested Resource

The *Serendipity Series* by Lyman Coleman.

The Last Word

It's hard to "get the ball rolling," to get a group present and involved (or re-involved) in a meeting. According to a principle of physics, overcoming inertia takes the most energy. The ideas for openings will help move a group from stop (arrival) to start (involvement in the meeting). The ideas for breaks are *battery chargers* when needed.

6.

Getting Acquainted/Getting to Know Group Members

Focus: finding ways to share our lives/tell our stories

Means: suggestions for enabling sharing in brief and safe ways

Remembering that the two purposes of every group are 1) getting the task done and 2) taking care of the relationships in the group or *group maintenance*, this chapter will deal with how to attend to the second stated purpose above, caring for the people in your group.

As with all matters concerning relationships, it is not what is said or done in itself that creates warmth and caring between people. It is the attitude or heart behind the words and behavior. This chapter offers more than *ice breaking* techniques. There are no canned ploys for "warming people up" and guaranteeing that the "players" will feel warmly accepted. What I am talking about here has to do with a facilitator being authentically concerned about each person in their group. *Genuine personal caring on the part of the facilitator helps to create and support right relationships in any group.* It is impossible to really care about someone without knowing them and it is impossible to really know a person without listening to "their story." Being aware of each person's life context makes it easier to understand and respect thoughts and feelings contributed to the group task. So it is important that the facilitator cares for group relationships by regularly, care-fully and safely enabling personal sharing, however brief, as part of every small group. It is just as important that the facilitator empowers the group with good listening skills both by modeling and by offering guidelines as appropriate. When a person is free to share appropriately and can count on being heard and respected (not judged or advised), trust and understanding creates a safe place for honest expression of thoughts and opinions.

Given the above, here are some suggestions for facilitating sharing and listening on a personal level within a group.

Guidelines

A. Prepare in Advance

1. Spend some time reflecting on the upcoming meeting. Consider the following factors before deciding what kind of "Getting to know you" or "Getting to know you better" exercise to include: type of group (young mother's support group? parish finances task force? Scripture study ministry team?) focus of meeting (getting the ministry started? conflict resolution? bringing closure?); numbers expected (a group of five can do processes that 65 cannot); facilities (how much room needed to move around); number of gatherings (one time or one of a series?); amount of meeting time available overall and specifically the amount available for the desired exercise.
2. Considering all of the above, decide the best process to use (short or long, light-hearted or in-depth, verbal or nonverbal, sharing with partners or with the whole group), any materials needed in advance and how your assistant can help.

B. Suggestions for Beginning—and Continuing

1. When a group begins a commitment for an extended period of time, give a good portion of the year's first meeting to "Getting to know you." Offer the goal of knowing, loving and serving God and one another in whatever task belongs to the group. Discuss the relationship between serving out of love and loving out of knowing. Serving God wholeheartedly then begins with spending time to seek God, to know God. Make the correlation to the human community. Serving

each other as group members and serving the group as a whole begins with knowing one another so as to love one another. Whatever the task of the group is, call them first to be signs of the kingdom as a group. Set before them the desire to be a model of loving relationships as well as to be a model of efficient achievement.

2. At the beginning of each subsequent meeting of a group committed for an extended period of time, build in a "Getting to know you better" exercise, however brief. Simply remind the group that people come before task in the group so that every meeting will include a brief sharing time. In the first few meetings it is helpful to find ways to use one another's names in some creative way with or without nametags.

3. If the meeting is a one time gathering, at least acknowledge the fact that everyone there is a person with a history that somehow led them to this meeting and you regret there not being enough time to share that history. Perhaps you could at least have them turn to one other person, share where they are from and why they came to this particular gathering.

4. At the conclusion of a group's commitment time, it is wise to include in the evaluation (or in addition to the evaluation) what gift the group members have given (see Chapter 10 on Closure).

Methods/Suggestions/Exercises

A. "Getting to Know You" exercises

1. Longer processes

a. Give each person an outline of a USA map (or give a blank piece of paper and ask each to sketch an outline from a sample you show. The telephone book offers a good model). Ask them to place an "X" where they were born and where they presently live. Then ask them to place an "X" (or some other more appropriate symbol) on significant places on their journeying that ultimately brought them to this Church, for this meeting. After marking all the most important places, connect them with a line. It is helpful to give them guidelines: don't make it just a travelogue; keep it to the most significant places on your journey—hopefully 4-6 places/people/events that helped shape your life in important ways; keep it safe— no need to disclose anything you are not comfortable with; when another is sharing their journeying, listen respectfully without interruption. Give the group 10 minutes to complete their map then ask them to share for another 5-10 minutes. If the group is small (4-8 people), have each share with the whole group. If the group is larger, ask each to find a partner, and share their journey with each other. When you think there has been enough time, check to see how many need more time and adjust. Give a warning that time is up in 5 minutes. When the group reassembles, follow up in some way.

Some suggestions are: have each person *introduce* their partner (name, where from and one significant thing that impressed them about their story); go around the circle, each one giving their name, where they're from originally and perhaps one interesting step on their journey which in some way contributed to being part of Church—and this group; go around the group, each giving their name, where they presently live and one feeling that came out of their time of sharing.

b. Give each person a simple drawing of a curving pathway (or have them draw their own using yours as a model). At one end of the path place a sign on a large post saying, "birth." At the other end of the path place a sign on a large post saying, "future." Place four or five other signs along the pathway and ask them to fill in a word or symbol to signify some significant crossroads on their life journey. Follow directions concerning time, process and followup.

c. Ask the group to divide into pairs after giving directions: Each person share with partner for five minutes each about the context of their lives (where born and raised, education and or career choices, family life, what kind of spiritual journey led them to the Church and to this meeting). After ten minutes, call the group back and go around the circle, each person introducing their partner with name, where originally from and one significant thing you learned about this person that will help make him/her a valuable group member.

2. Shorter processes/exercises

   a. Ask each to share their name, where they were originally from, and four significant facts about their current life (e.g. married to Ray, have seven grown children, am a teacher and a writer, love babies).

   b. Ask each to share their name, where they were originally from and to name those with whom they spend the most time.

   c. Ask each to give their name and a 1 or 2 minute context of their life (facilitator model with own information concerning where born and raised, what she or he has spends the bulk of their life doing, living situation (retired? empty nest? newly married? children?)

   d. Ask each to share their name, where they were originally from, why they are Christian and why they have chosen to be part of this group.

B. "Getting to Know You Better" Exercises

1. Longer processes/exercises

   a. Sharing stories/memories from the growing up years:

      What was special about your grandparents?

      Share something special about Mom and Dad (bring snapshot?).

      Name your siblings, your birth order, its significance.

      How would others describe you as a child? an adolescent?

What warm memory stands out from your childhood?

Describe your favorite childhood home. Why special?

Share the childhood playmates and game you liked the most.

Describe your favorite holiday, book or movie from your youth.

What do you remember about your first day of high school?

Share what you remember about your first date.

Who was your hero/heroine in your youth? (and why?)

Share about a family trip/outing that was special.

Share a humorous embarrassing moment (that you are comfortable sharing).

What were your nicknames growing up? Did you like/dislike any of them?

Share a warm memory of your youthful experience of God.

Who was your favorite teacher as a youth? Why?

Share your memories of your high school graduation.

Who would you call "holy" (walked with God) from your youth?

What memory from your teen years won't you tell your own teenagers?

b. Sharing memories/stories from the adult years:

Share one memory when you felt very close to God.

What is the kindest thing a stranger ever did for you?

Share a story about how the Church supported you in a time of need.

What do you remember about your first job as an adult?

Describe your oldest friend. Why the continued connection?

What is the best lesson you learned the first year of marriage?

Tell a story about a lesson a specific child has taught you?

Who was there for you when you needed someone the most?

Share a warm or humorous memory concerning your children (or any child).

Share a story about a crazy or risky adventure you took.

Tell about a great vacation you had and what made it great.

Share how one of your children/grandchildren honored you.

Share one blessing and/or pain from this past week.

2. Shorter ways of sharing

a. Sharing likes/dislikes, interests, preferences:

Describe what you like to do in your spare time.

What is your favorite prayer and/or hymn? Why?

Where do you like to sit in Church? Why there?

Do you have a *pet peeve*? What is it?

If it was free, where would you go on vacation? Why there?

What do you hope your children will remember about you?

What music would you like sung at your funeral?

What animal are you most like today?

What tree are you most like today?

What flower are you most like today?

Name a contemporary faith model who inspires you.

What do you consider a perfect prayer setting?

Name some of the places/activities you find really lifegiving.

What is your favorite movie and why?

Which relative would you like to spend more time with? Why?

What book would you most want to read again and why?

Do you have an old family *motto* that you have passed on?

b. Sharing ideas, values and dreams:

What question would you like to ask God face to face today?

What virtue do you think is key to family peace?

With whom would you most like to experience reconciliation?

What "saint" would you most like to invite to dinner?

If your work was all done, what would you like to do?

What dream of yours would you finance if you won the lottery?

Where is your most treasured place to be?

What would you like to be "when you grow up"?

What principle would you really *fight for*?

When do you experience your greatest sense of wellbeing?

If you were guaranteed a "yes" what request would you make?

Suggested Resource

Ceating Small Faith Communities by Arthur Baronowski.

The Last Word

Most people are anxiously awaiting your knock on their door so they can ask you in to sup with them. Take a chance. Knock. Enter ever so gently. Sit and listen ever so respectfully. Get to know and love each other more.

7.

Using Effective Discussion Leader Techniques

Focus: skills that facilitate a good discussion

Means: checklists of do's and don'ts

Facilitating is an art of using skills with heart to create a climate of comfort and safety in groups. There are discussion leader techniques that help build bridges of trust and respect and enable healthy discussions. Perhaps the basic element is the facilitator's own authenticity and freedom to be his or her own self while moving the discussion along in ordinary and challenging situations and with difficult people.

Techniques that move a discussion along in ordinary situations

A. *DO* begin the group comfortably and ON TIME. Pull the chairs in close (if it's a small group) so that there is good eye contact and a comfortable closeness. Begin on time with greetings that are welcoming and authentic (I want to begin by welcoming you to. . .). If the group is large, use music, a bell, or a microphone-amplified greeting/song to pull the stragglers in then just BEGIN on time—again with simple welcoming words.

   DON'T keep waiting for late-comers or stragglers in the room before starting because that implicitly trains people to be late and insults (and often infuriates) those who paid a price to be on time.

B. *DO* prepare and use an agenda. *DO* "keep on track" by first determining the goal of your meeting time and then preparing an agenda. Determine in advance what your goal and objectives are. Then, plan the agenda. For instance, when facilitating a group meeting to plan a parish Oktoberfest, know that the goal for the planning meeting is to implement the goal and objectives agreed upon by the parish council. Given this, a sample agenda for the planning meeting might be:

Goal:

to involve as many parish groups as possible; to have a variety of activities/booths; to share any profit with the Grief Ministry

Agenda:

1-30 minutes Welcome, introductions. Share an experience of community fun

30-60 minutes—Share goal and proposed objectives; discuss improvements/additions.

60-70 minutes—Break

70-120 minutes—Brainstorm ways to implement objectives; prioritize the best ideas according to agreed upon criteria (money, time, resources); agree on delegation of responsibilities.

Whether you use such a simple outline or prepare one with even more detailed items and times, remember to be flexible. Think of your agenda as a sturdy skeleton to be fleshed out or a friendly framework to fill in or even a pliable plan from which to deviate RATHER than a demanding dictator controlling every minute.

DON'T arrive at any meeting without having the goal in mind or an agenda written down. Do not, however, be a slave to the agenda you have prepared. Rather, adapt as necessary, in order to reach your goal and objectives.

C. *DO* keep track of time during the meeting. Clearly state the meeting length at the beginning of a small group. This gives someone who has to leave early a chance to alert the group. His/her departure will be less disruptive and the group may decide to rearrange the agenda (or one person make a commitment to fill in for what was missed). Be flexible about following each planned item on your formal or informal agenda. Use good judgment based on balancing task and relationship purposes (Chapter 2) when concerned about time. Remember that good ministry is a response to authentic need. When it is time to move on, a direct and simple approach is "I'm concerned about the time because we have ________ ________ meeting time left. Are you ready to wrap this item up?"

DON'T be either a slave to stated times on the agenda or careless about time. Balancing between these two extremes is a challenge. If this is an area of strain for you, ask for help from your assistant or another group member who has a good sense of time.

D. *DO* understand the use of specific skills that facilitate a good discussion. Some of these discussion skills are:

- initiating some movement forward when the discussion isn't moving by *defining terms* ("I'd like to take the word ________________, and see if we agree on what it means. What is your sense of this word?"); by *making some suggestion* ("What's the first thing that comes to mind when you think of this subject?"); by *trying out an idea* ("I'm guessing that there are a lot of feelings surrounding this issue. I suggest we go around the circle and give a one word *feeling* response, before further discussion.")
- offering information/opinions/facts/suggestions or eliciting the same from other group members ("I read in last night's paper that. . . .", "I'd like to go around the circle and gather any facts anyone knows about this issue. If you don't have anything to add, just pass.")
- building on another's thoughts ("I like what you said about . . ., Mary. That's been my experience also. . . .")
- clarifying and elaborating ("I think I can clear up that point with an example . . . (or "Does anyone have an idea that would help us clarify?"); I'd like to add one thought . . . (or "Would anyone else like to add a thought?")

- summarizing ("I think we are at a point of pulling this together so I would like to try and sum up what we have discussed so far and see if we are ready to move on. Would someone be willing to try and sum up our discussion on this point?")
- gatekeeping/inviting participants into the discussion ("Robyn, would you like to add anything to this discussion right now?," "Starting with Joan, I would like to go around the circle and given everyone a chance to respond to this question. If you need more time to think, pass.")
- harmonizing/honoring differing points of view ("So Joe believes that . . . I think I hear that Jane's viewpoint is very different. Thank you both for sharing your opinions.")
- bringing in humor—laughing appropriately—helping the group to *lighten up* ("We have been talking so seriously since we began today that I would like to take a breather and share a cartoon on this subject." or "Anyone know a good joke on this subject?")

DON'T think that it is always up to you to respond to every situation with the perfect skill. The facilitator is a group member and every group member carries responsibility for having a good meeting (though in the beginning the facilitator may have to do more than his/her fair share). *Give away* your extra responsibility as soon as possible by asking for help and encouraging the participation of others. When others contribute, use the above skills and make sure that you affirm both the person and the gift.

Techniques that intervene in challenging situations

A. *DO* deal with intrusions firmly and directly.

- Acknowledge the late-comers (if the group is small or in the home) with a simple nod/greeting, suggesting the person get filled in at coffee break or after the meeting.
- Make an agreement about the phone (if the meeting is in the home or a conference room with a phone). For an ongoing meeting situation, agree on a signal

that each could communicate for those who would need to contact them in an emergency (one ring then hang up and call again?). If, for some important reason it is necessary to receive phone calls, agree on who will answer it and take messages.

DON'T interrupt the flow of the meeting by stopping everything and starting over—and over—and over with each interruption.

B. When time is especially crunched, the agenda is unfinished and there is a high level of anxiety. . . .

DO acknowledge the limitations of time, your inability to complete the agenda in the time left, your concern and any sensed anxiety in others. ("I am frustrated and very aware that we are almost out of time and have not attended to everything planned. The items left are . . . Which items do you think a subcommittee can finish? . . . Volunteers? . . . Which items can be postponed to the next meeting? . . .")

DON'T pretend there is no problem and no feelings surrounding it. Be honest and nondefensive. Do not run the meeting overtime to make up for the problem (unless the whole group wants to).

C. When there seems to be no response to the discussion as you ask for input or reaction. . . .

DO try the ideas under *initiating* above. Try eliciting a stream-of-consciousness response ("Let's take the word, ____________________ . Say the first thought that comes to mind when you hear this word."), either spontaneously or in round-robin order. When going around the circle in the round-robin order, do acknowledge that some personalities need more process time ("If you need more time to think, just pass"). Acknowledge that some silence is good and you will allow for it.

DON'T wait until the silence is uncomfortable. Don't fill in the gaps yourself.

D. When the discussion is deteriorating with heated polarization between members. . . .

DO acknowledge the reality of opposite stalemated viewpoints and your discomfort with trying to get agreement rather than to understand one another. Paraphrase what you hear each one saying. Get them to agree to disagree and suggest moving on. ("I hear Dan's viewpoint is ____________ and Jim's is just the opposite. I am uncomfortable with trying to get an agreement. I suggest you agree to disagree so we can move on.") Possibly the group could agree to reflect on the subject and return to it at the next meeting.

DON'T get into the argument and take sides or keep silent until the whole group is very uncomfortable.

E. In the aftermath of a tragedy or traumatizing event in a group member's life. . . .

DO acknowledge the reality of the pain. Give the person space to share IF they want to. Enable empathetic listening ("None of us can take your pain away but I want you to know we care about you and want to simply be with you in your pain.") You could take a minute for silent prayer or a familiar rote prayer before moving on.

DON'T either carry on as if nothing happened nor focus all the group's attention on that member for the whole meeting time. Don't give or allow advice giving ("Thank you for your concern. There will be another time for sharing wisdom on practical matters. Right now it is important to just let you know we care.")

Techniques that deal with Difficult People

A. With the dominator who talks too much. . . .

DO intervene in a carefully timed way. When the dominator takes a breath, use authentic words—and touch—if nothing else works and the person is close to you ("Jane, I see you have done a lot of thinking on this subject. Thank you for sharing. Anyone else want to add your thoughts?"). You can also try paraphrasing what was said (see Chapter 3) and then again, immediately invite others into the discussion.

DON'T either wait too long to intervene (or a group anger will build) nor ignore this overtalkative person's real contributions (or you will lose a group member).

B. With the negator who really puts down ideas and/or people. . . .

DO acknowledge his/her statements as opinions and invite others to share their opinions ("Ellen, you seem to have a strong reaction to this issue. There are probably others here who feel differently. Any other opinions?") If the person's negativity is focused on a person it is usually masked as negative humor, state your discomfort and change direction in some way. ("I am really uncomfortable with negative humor.") Then change the direction of the discussion.

DON'T ignore negativity. It de-energizes any group and perpetuates difficult behavior.

C. With the very quiet or shy member who is noncontributing. . . .

DO be gentle and affirming of the person's value while waiting for him/her to feel safe about participating ("I would like to give everyone a chance to participate who wants to respond to this question"—look at nonparticipating person briefly.) If the person does respond be as specifically and authentically affirming as possible. The reasons for not contributing are sometimes fear and lack of confidence or for some the need to listen a long while before getting involved in the discussion. It is helpful to remember the reasons behind the behavior in order to respond in effective ways. This is a good situation in which to use a *whip-around* process because it gives everyone an OPPORTUNITY to participate and that is more important that actual participation. ("I would like to start a whip-around process on this issue before moving on, or to get the discussion started. We will start to my left and go around the circle for a quick one sentence response. If you need more time to think, just say 'pass'.") Be patient!

DON'T pressure or coax the person to participate nor be *gushy* when they do. This will only decrease the person's level of safety. Do not be impatient. Give the person time and opportunity.

D. With the *Court Jester* who jokes inappropriately. . . .

DO be honest about how his/her behavior affects you. ("John, I am distracted by your joking. I don't know when to take you seriously.") This might need to be done privately.

DON'T laugh at the jokester out of nervousness, embarrassment, or out of not knowing how to respond. This will perpetuate his/her behavior that is inappropriate.

E. With the rambler who easily gets off the subject with ruminations and irrelevancies. . . .

DO intervene at the first opportunity in order to get back to the topic. ("Thank you for your sharing, Fay. I would like to call us back to the topic. . . .") If necessary, give your own reflections on the topic while the other group members get their thoughts together. Another method is to catch onto a word as it goes by and relate it to the subject. ("I'm glad you mentioned that. . . . It brings us back to the subject we began with. . . .")

DON'T just watch the group members get increasingly uncomfortable while the rambler eats up all the group time. It is not wise to either *put up with* or to *put down* the rambler but rather to effect a refocusing.

Suggested Resource

Dealing with Difficult People by Charles J. Keating.

The Last Word

Remember that the best way to deal with difficulties in a group is to prevent them from arising by understanding group process, using good communication skills and creating a warm and safe climate (Chapters 1-4). Do handle difficulties that arise with objectivity and empathy, encouraging all the group members to share responsibility for both task and relationships in the group. Ask for help especially from God who is faithful to give you all the tools needed when you answer the call to facilitate.

8.

Enabling Group Prayer

Focus: prayerful prayerways

Means: ways to focus, to gently elicit communal prayer

The most important way to enable prayer for others is to be a prayerful person yourself. No technique, method or formula can substitute for the model of a person who is "at home" with God. The prayerfulness of that person is *THE* single most important factor in enabling prayer for others. Whatever words or means are used to lead prayer, the facilitator's prayerful spirit in itself becomes an invitation to pray. *PRAYERFULNESS IS THE MOST AUTHENTIC WAY OF INVITING OTHERS INTO COMFORTABLE PRAYER-WAYS.*

Given the above, here are some suggestions for leading prayer in a group.

Process

A. Prepare in advance

1. Find a quiet place and take time to focus yourself: Find a comfortable position and relax your body; take a deep breath and exhale slowly; close your eyes and be quietly present to the Spirit within you. Invite God to commune with you and ask for the grace to respond in faith. 'Waste' some time just quietly being with God and remembering God's promise over and over in Scripture: "I will be with you." Ex-

pect inspiration, wisdom for the best prayerway for your upcoming meeting of God's people.

2. Spend time reflecting on the upcoming meeting. Consider the goal and objectives, specific interest group of people, expected numbers attending, meeting room available and its assets and limitations regarding the climate for different prayer forms, how much time you want to build in for prayer and when in the meeting specific prayer would be most appropriate.

3. Gather your resource possibilities (bible, books, music, etc.) and outline your plan for leading prayer. Put the finished plan on a large notecard indicating time allotments (if lengthy), resources needed. Title the card according to time, place in meeting, group name (e.g., 5 minute Scripture Introduction to Parish Council meeting). NB: modify time or directions on the card immediately after your experience then file as one of your resources when planning to lead another prayertime.

B. Onsite Preparation/Enabling/Closure Ideas

1. Prepare the environment in any way necessary to create a climate more conducive to prayer—depending on your chosen prayer form (darken the room and light a candle for example if you are opening the meeting with a meditation; give directions for moving the chairs out of the way if closing with a prayer circle).

2. Take time to center yourself, to focus on being consciously present to God before you call the group to prayer. Remember, your model of genuine prayerfulness is the secret ingredient in enabling others to pray.

3. Make a simple statement of invitation to prayer, giving directions for group participation in any way needed. Lead the group to quiet and focus themselves. Wait for a few moments of silence before beginning. Don't be afraid of some silence during the prayer time especially if leading spontaneous prayer.

If there seems to be confusion or lack of participation during the prayer time consider restating a direction or giving encouragement with an "I" statement.

4. Gently and clearly, bring the prayer time to a closure ("Be with us God as we now continue our meeting empowered by your Spirit, Amen.") ("Please join me as we conclude our prayer time with the Lord's Prayer. . . .")
5. Take a few moments for transition into business if prayer time is at the beginning or during the meeting (so as to model that prayer is not perfunctory, or just another item on the agenda)

Content (or Prayerways)

A. Focus on Scripture

1. At the beginning or end of a meeting prayerfully read an uplifting and appropriate Scripture (or excerpts from a scripture) then reflect in silence.
   a. From the Hebrew Scriptures (Old Testament)

      Psalms 8, 24, 46, 63, 660-67, 84, 95-100, 111, 118, 135-136, 148-150

      Ex 33: 12-17, Nb 6:24-26, 1 Kings 19:9-13, Dt 6:1-9; Sirach 2:7-18, Is 40:3-5, Is 55:1-3, Is 58: 5-11, Ez 37:3-14, Daniel 3:52-90.

   b. From the Christian Scriptures (New Testament)

      The Gospels: Mk 6:34-44, 12:28-31; Mt 5:3-12, 6:26-34, 7:7-11, 11:28-30, 28:16-20; Lk 1:46-55, 1:68-79, 6:20-26, 11:1-13; John 13:13-17, 13:34-35, 15:9-17

      The Letters: Rom 12:9-21; 1 Cor 13:1-7; Eph 3:14-21; Phil 1:3-6, 2:5-11, 4:5-9; Col 2:6-7, 3:12-17; 1 Jn 4:7-13

2. For a lengthier and more in depth use of Scripture consider the collasio method.

a. Select a colorful passage of scripture such as one of the stories of healing or miracles in the gospels and read it through out loud slowly and with animation. Then enable the group to walk through the story with you recreating the scenes by imagining the sights, sounds, smells, and feelings.

b. Reread the passage followed by a time of eliciting the different messages personally gleaned from hearing the word.

c. Ask the group to close their eyes this time and listen without reading along, to listen carefully to the passage as the word of God and to then respond with short, simple prayers of the heart. Facilitator can simply model one word or phrase prayers of thanksgiving (for instance after the story of the healing of the blind man at Bethsaida in Mk 8:22-25 is read 3 times, a model response might be: "Thank you God for persistence—mine and yours." Then invite others to add their words of thanksgiving (or praise or petition or intercession) resulting from listening to this passage.

3. Try a creative reading of Scripture called *jamming* (for small groups who can sit in a circle and read in 'round robin' order). Select an inspiring scripture passage of reasonable length. Type out and duplicate for each participant or make sure everyone has the same translation. Explain the directions ahead of time explaining that the goal of this prayerway in particular is to become hearers of the word:

   a. Round robin reading of the passage, beginning with the facilitator and each reading to the punctuation mark. Provide a moment of silence at end of passage.

   b. Round robin reading of the same passage, beginning with facilitator, each one *giving* the words to the next reader by stopping at any place other than the punctuation mark. Encourage each to be listening to the word so attentively that they can immediately pick up the next words in a smooth and prayerful manner. Provide a few moments of silence at the end.

c. Round robin reading of the same passage, beginning with the person next to the facilitator (in order to model "taking" the words from the next person as the Spirit moves). Each in turn listens and begins to read, initially 'voicing over' the previous reader for a few words before that reader becomes silent. Provide a few moments of silence at end.

d. Facilitator appoints someone to begin reading the same passage after which anyone can spontaneously take the next words in the passage (as above except *NOT* in round robin order). Encourage the group to: allow for silences—not to rush in to fill space; feel comfortable if a number of people choose to read the same words; possibly repeat the same important or personally powerful word quietly and prayerfully. Provide a few moments of silence at the end.

e. Facilitator can choose to read the same passage one last time, leaving space after each thought segment for spontaneous prayers of the heart—either vocally or silently. End with an "Amen."

4. Use a scripture story as basis for a guided meditation.

   a. Choose a colorful passage, one that is graphic enough that an artist could paint the scenes or actors could dramatize it. The calming of the storm in Luke 8:22-25 is a good example.

   b. Read the passage once slowly and prayerfully.

   c. Ask the group to relax and focus, to find a comfortable position, breathe deeply and exhale slowly; close eyes and be quietly present to the Spirit within guiding each to new insights. Allow a few moments of silence.

   d. Ask that each one imagine that they are part of the scene described—feel the boat under them, the wind howling, the water sloshing over the side of the boat, the fear that rises up in their heart.

e. Ask them to connect with whatever else is going on in their life that brings on the same feeling of fear. Ask them to clearly name the stormy area in their lives and realize they are not alone in that vulnerable position. Jesus is with them right in the midst of that scary place.

f. Ask them then to imagine that Jesus is as available to them as he was to those in the boat. Have them *wake up* Jesus and ask him to help to calm the storm in their life. Encourage them to be quietly and expectantly present to the response of Jesus that will touch their fear with understanding.

g. Provide a time of silence to experience this.

h. Bring the meditation to a closure with a short prayer of thanksgiving and an invitation to return to the room and be present to the group once more

5. Lead a communal reflection on Scripture.

   a. Use a resource such as God's Word Today, Share the Word, or the Read and Pray series. It would be especially helpful for groups committed to meeting regularly to use one small section each time as an ongoing more systematic formation in scripture followed by a time of prayer. You could use the prayer starter suggestions offered in the pamphlet to elicit spontaneous prayer, or to serve as model for each one writing their own prayer response. Those who feel comfortable then could read their response prayerfully as a closing prayer. Another way to respond to the word of God (the essence of prayer) is to draw, paint or sculpt your response while a meditative, instrumental audio tape is playing. Sharing them in silence is optional.

Other focuses or prayerways

1. Enabling communal vocal prayer

   a. Elicit a chorus of praise: Ask the group to think of their favorite three names for God. Give them a few moments, then ask them to reverently and prayerfully say one name each time you lead them (with a word, soft bell, hand motion like a conductor's) (example: "We the people of God call your name." "We the people of God love your name ______________." "We the people of God praise your name ______________________. Amen"

   b. Elicit a litany of thanksgiving: Ask each to think of one thing they are grateful for that can be expressed in a few words, (for a good husband/healthy children/fulfilling ministry/a new day). Elicit or suggest a communal response such as "Gracious God, we thank you." Facilitator begin by offering a statement of gratitude ("For everyone who could be with us today." Then motion the group to respond with the agreed upon common response "Gracious God, we thank you." When you sense that those who want to have expressed their thanksgiving, give a concluding statement ("For all these expressed and unexpressed prayers, Dear God, we say, Amen.")

   c. Direct antiphonal formal or sung prayer: divide the group in half each with an appointed facilitator to pool the group as to their favorite formal prayers, Psalms or contemporary songs. Have each group choose one or more songs and/or formal prayers and then report that choice to the leader of the meeting. Leader decide where to divide each prayer and song in half. Have the group who chose it begin a song and/or prayer and say or sing half of it with the other group completing it.

   d. Elicit a prayer of lament and groaning: acknowledge the release that often comes with a groan. Remind them of Paul's statement in scripture that all creation groans to be set free. Ask them to think of what is holding them in bondage, of what causes their spirit to groan when they think about it, to name it silently and clearly in their own mind. Remind them that it is physiologically releasing to groan. Ask them to join all creation longing to be set free, to groan for "all the ways you want to be authentically free and yet are stuck." Encourage them to groan for one minute. Suggest handwringing or headholding as being natural to lamenters (as in the psalms of Lament such as Ps 13). Conclude with an "Amen" said with power three times.

e. Elicit a whisper of petition: ask each to think of three needs they have that they would like to remind God about. Give them a few minutes to reflect and name them to themselves. Ask them to whisper one need all at the same time after you intone, "Lord, hear our prayer." Do this three times.

Use other sources as you would scripture—as initial inspiration, as invitation to respond in prayer (in silence or vocally, in clay or paint, in poetry or dance.) Good sources might be: books like Song of the Bird or Meditations with Meister Eckhart; tapes like Dawn, or Environments (see bibliography); inspriational, photos or videos.

2. Enabling Body Prayer

a. Lead the group to feel their pulse (wrist or neck) or to place their hand on their chest in order to feel their lungs expand and deflate. Elicit feelings about the simple miracles of life that we tend to take for granted. Focus. Feel. Suggest gratitude prayers.

b. Lead a moving prayer of praise as in the Doxology (Glory Be to God, Amen). Ask the group to stand and practice the movements you show them: elicit what would be a natural expression of joy and exuberance that could accompany the word, "Glory" (raised hands, lifted head). Ask them then to let their body hear and respond to their words in praising God. Lead them to say or sing "Glory be to our God. . . ." while raising both hands as high as they can, lifting the head and stretching the body upward. Pause. When saying or singing, "And to Jesus," bring arms down and cross over chest, lower head and eyes. Pause. When saying or singing, "And to the Holy Spirit," stretch arms out to both sides, connecting hands or locking arms with people on either side. Pause. When saying or singing, "Amen," keep arms or hands connected and bow together from the waist (the Grand Bow). Pause. Call that a practice and repeat the process prayerfully.

c. Lead the group in a stretch and groan prayer similar to section 1.d above but ask the group to stand, move apart and stretch in every direction while you name some of our generic sins as human beings ("for making promises I don't keep, for not taking good enough care of my body, for all the times I neglected someone I care about. . . .") or general problem areas specific to that particular group's interest.

d. Lead the group in a standing ovation for themselves or a sitting and footstamping ovation for God (complete with whistles if a youth group). This is good at the end of an uplifting meeting (prayer is not always subdued).

e. Lead the group into offering the Kiss of Peace very reverently and slowly to at least two people. Have them stand, get centered, in touch with the peace within them. THEN ask them to consciously share that peace with another using a firm handshake or authentic hug, and good eye contact as they bless the other with their own brief words of peace or the traditional words for the Kiss of Peace.

f. Sing or say the "Jesus Prayer" (or any other simple repetition prayer with gestures that match the words. Suggestion: When you say "Lord, Jesus Christ," slowly raise hands from hanging at your sides to stretched upward, palms up, by the time you say the next words, "Son of God." As you begin the next phrase, "Have Mercy on me" bring hands down and together, folded in a traditional supplication pose, with head and eyes down. As you say the last words, "and heal me" (a modification, hold yourself as if to hug yourself, hands on opposite shoulders).

g. Try a squeeze prayer: ask the group to sit or stand in small circles and join hands (make sure each is in a comfortable position). Ask them to close their eyes, to breathe deeply and to focus on the power and love of God within them. Give them a moment to feel this. Ask them to focus on sharing that love and power of God with each other by 'passing it around' the circle by squeezing the hand on their other side as soon as their hand is squeezed. Suggest they image that love as golden rope holding them together as it weaves around the circle. Facilitator begin the hand squeeze going in one direction. Keep it going until you sense it's time to end then quietly say, "Amen." Another way to use this is to add verbal prayers at the squeeze signal (when you feel your hand squeezed, add your word or phrase of praise, thanksgiving, petition etc., or *pass* by simply squeezing the hand of the next person so they will get a signal for their turn).

h. Provide small vials of blessed oil for each person. Lead the group to reflect on the part of their body used most in their particular ministry (examples could be: mouth for a teacher; hands for a eucharistic minister or mom; heart for a counselor). Ask the group to form pairs and have each partner ask the other to bless that part of their body by making the sign of the cross with oil while expressing a simple prayer (like, "I bless you in the name of our gracious God. May your hands continue to bless and comfort those you touch").

i. Ask the group to stand and pray by very slowly and reverently singing, clapping and swaying together in rhythm to the spiritual, "This little light of mine."

Suggested Resource

Pray Always by Edward Hays.

The Last Word

God has a vested interest in teaching you how to pray. Ask for help then just begin.

9.

Keeping the Group Growing/Improving

Focus: naming the strengths (what is working) and the weaknesses (what is not working) in the program, process and relationships

Means: manageable and measurable processes to evaluate each group situation

Evaluation is vital for the health of any group or process. Facilitators might believe this but seldom or ineffectively enable participants to assess the strengths and weaknesses in their group relationships and activities. Whether your small group is a parish council, a paid parish staff, a woman's guild or a few volunteers training to facilitate a Scripture study, it is crucial to include regular evaluation. Group members who give and receive honest feedback about process, program and relationships guarantee improvement. This is because such a group implicitly commits to growth by learning to honestly and openly communicate. With such communication, the facilitator can effectively modify or amplify procedures or plans, deal with problems and eliminate roadblocks. On the other hand, without regular feedback, problems escalate, mistakes get repeated, misunderstandings go underground (hanging around to subvert progress), and good work or ideas often remain unrecognized and undeveloped.

The reasons many facilitators ignore or shortchange the need to build in regular evaluation has to do with 1) fear (of pain because past experiences of evaluation were demoralizing/diminishing in the manner in which they were carried out), 2) anger (that is probably suppressed or detoured) over some injustice related to the content or to nonreciprocity in the process during and after previous experiences, and 3) ignorance of manageable ways of incorporating evaluation as a basic tool of group development.

Guidelines

A. When dealing with interpersonal relations within the group (including between facilitator and assistant), use the feedback process. Feedback gives constructive information that helps another person become aware of how their words and behavior are perceived by and affect you. Learn how to give feedback in a way that will not be threatening to the other person. Learn how to receive feedback in an open, nondefensive manner.

   1. When giving feedback, focus on what a video camera could capture (specific, observable behavior and its effect on you) not on a critique of another's motivation, intent or culpability. "When you respond quickly and at length to most discussion questions, I am grateful for your input but when most others haven't shared, I feel concerned that some who want to share won't have the opportunity. I need to ask you to stay aware of that and help make space for all to share."

   2. When receiving feedback, focus on being open and trying to understand rather than to defend or blame. Do this by paraphrasing or summarizing what you think the other is saying. "You are suggesting that I take more time before I respond and perhaps to be briefer so that everyone gets into the discussion. I'll try."

B. When deciding in general about evaluation processes (which one, how, when, etc.) intended to critique content and process, prepare well in advance and do appropriate follow-up work.

1. Prepare in advance

   a. Spend time reflecting on upcoming meetings. Consider the focus, whether it's a single meeting or a series (if so, which place in the series), facilities, numbers expected, and overall meeting plan.

   b. Considering all of the above, decide: 1) the best place to integrate an evaluation process into the meeting (focus of the whole meeting? short processes interspersed throughout the meeting? part of the meeting wrapup?); 2) the best method/process to use (short or long, verbal or nonverbal, written or active); 3) any materials that need advance preparation; 4) how your assistant will help you keep track of time so you don't let the evaluation process slide (especially if this is a new discipline for you); and 5) *when* you will elicit feedback from your assistant regarding your facilitation (What did I do well today? One suggestion for improvement).

2. Follow-up

   a. Make sure that you pay attention to the information received from your evaluation process. If you use a short process then you and your assistant need to reflect on the feedback after the meeting to see which ideas seem workable and able to quickly improve the group process/work/relationships. Decide which ideas need more time and group involvement to develop. For suggestions that are simple and immediately possible, discuss when, how and who will implement each.

   b. At the next group meeting make sure you acknowledge the helpfulness of their suggestions in general. Share which specific concerns you are addressing and which suggestions you are immediately implementing. If there are more complex or questionable suggestions respond either by 1) offering alternate proposals for consideration, discussion, decision and possibly a trial period (for the sake of time and particularly if you detect resistance) and 2) *brainstorming* an important problem for which no solution seems apparent. To make this work, set the ground rules of ideating without judging (elicit suggestions/possible changes freely without allowing evaluative responses). Record every idea for later consideration according to agreed upon criteria (either decided at that meeting, a later meeting or by the leaders responsible for the group).

c. *Attending to the group's suggestions and taking tangible action is the best way to affirm group members and involve them in taking responsibility for continued growth and improvement.*

Methods

A. Quick processes

1. Nonverbal

a. Ask the group to evaluate the meeting (or some part of it) on a scale of 1-10 (10 is high/excellent and one is low/very poor). Ask each to raise their hands as the appropriate number is named. Facilitator call out the numbers 1-10 and note the hands that are up. Follow up by going once around the group (if small enough) to give each a chance to briefly explain what was needed to have earned a "ten."

b. Ask each to show by the height of their hand (high = best and low = worst) how each thought the meeting went. Follow up with once around the group (if small enough) for a one word or phrase explanation.

c. At the beginning of a meeting, pass out half sheets of paper to each. Ask them to draw a large smiley face on one side and large frowning face on the other. At different parts of the meeting (if there ARE distinctive activities) or at the end of the meeting, ask each to hold up the appropriate face in response to questions such as: How do you feel about the tasks accomplished and /or decisions made at our meeting today? How did you feel about the warmth or level of caring expressed among us today? How did you feel about the effectiveness of the processes used?

2. Verbal

   a. If the group is small enough, go around the group and ask each to name one strength of that day's meeting. Go around a second time and ask each to name one weakness in that day's meeting (can ask to name the most helpful part and least helpful part). Ask each to limit their comments to one sentence.

   b. Elicit a list of typical feeling words. Ask each to "trust their gut" and spontaneously name what they are feeling with one word. When no one else is responding, use their feeling words to ask open ended questions like: "Some are feeling frustrated because . . .? Some are feeling relieved because . . .? Lead them to briefly 'fill in the blanks'."

   c. Lead the group to imagine repeating the same meeting after each one answers two questions: 1) If we were to repeat this meeting another time, what one thing would you want to do exactly the same, or "What I really liked . . . ." If we were to repeat this meeting another time, what one thing would you definitely want to do differently?

3. Written

   a. Have printed slips of paper ready to hand out during the last few minutes of every meeting. Ask open ended questions on each and leave a small amount of room to complete each sentence. Example: One specific and very helpful/effective part of today's meeting was ____________________.

   The least helpful/effective part of today's meeting was ______________________________.

   One suggestion for improvement is ____________.

b. Give the group five minutes only. Collect before ending the meeting.

c. Pass out half sheets of paper at the end of the meeting/class. Dictate or write on a blackboard/butcher paper the following open ended statements for each participant to complete and hand in before leaving:

I liked ______________________________

I learned ______________________________

I suggest ______________________________

d. Pass out half sheets of paper at the beginning of a meeting/class. Ask each person to put a plus sign (+) at the top of one side and a minus sign (-) at the top of the other side. Ask them to jot down parts of the meeting that they feel good—or not good about—on the appropriate side of the sheet as the meeting/class progresses. Collect before ending.

e. Have printed slips of paper available as each enters the room. Alert them at the beginning of the meeting that at the end they will be asked to rate on a scale of 1-10: tasks accomplished/decisions made ______________________ ; processes used ________________ ; caring atmosphere felt ____________________ at today's meeting.

B. Longer Processes

1. Written

a. Give each person paper and crayons. Ask each to draw a configuration of the group after showing them what a "model" group would look like (many different shapes of equal size equidistant from each other in a circle, all focused on something in the center of the circle). Suggest they use different shapes/symbols and their placement to indicate how each sees 1) the group's relationship to each other, and 2) the group's ability to focus on a common task. It is helpful to also use color to indicate feelings about the group (suggest they just trust their inner sense of which color represents which emotion). If this is a group of facilitators (such as in a Renew program or large Scripture study with many discussion groups) then each one does a configuration of the small group they facilitate. Otherwise, have each evaluate the group that is present. Allow some thinking time while playing meditative music and suggest silence during the exercise. Plan a generous amount of time for sharing the drawings. Instead of having the draw-er explain, suggest the group looks and responds with feelings and insights before the draw-er says anything. This process is especially good for relationship-focused or support groups that have been together for quite awhile.

b. Give the group paper and crayons and ask them to give a 'weather report' of today's meeting. Elicit what symbols the weather forecaster uses on the TV weather map. Ask the group to use these and/or other symbols to indicate their sense of the meeting just finished. When done ask each to write phrases next to each symbol to explain why that symbol was chosen. When done, ask each to write at the bottom of the page what they could have done differently to improve the "weather" for that day.

2. Active

a. Lead the group to evaluate via 'body sculpting'. Ask the group to stand and gather in a large circle. Form a group of 6-8 in the center for a demonstration. Begin by asking them to hold hands in a relaxed manner, to form a circle and to focus on the center of the circle. Offer this as one model of an ideal group (elicit why: connected, equal, focused). Ask them to watch as you move people around to form a live sculpture that describes a more real or typical configuration of a group. Without a lot of talking, the facilitator then *sculpts* each person in the demonstration group.

Show group configuration by *molding* each person's body stance, distance from each other (or possibly even distance from the whole group), hand connection (or lack of), facial expression (or lack of) and where each person's focus is. "Freeze" each in place as you finish them. When completed, elicit from the observers this demo group's strengths and weaknesses. Elicit possible problem areas. Ask each facilitator to choose and sculpt six or eight people to represent their small group configuration. This process works best at a ministry team meeting composed of facilitators all of whom lead small discussion groups as part of an ongoing series.

b. Lead the group to do 'body voting' on a continuum of 1-10. Walk to a spot on one side of the room, designating it as the lowest end (rating poor) of a continuum of 1-10. Walk from there to the other side of the room indicating where 10 (rating excellent) is. Ask each to listen to each question and then walk to the spot on the continuum that matches their rating. Ask questions appropriate to the type of meeting. For instance, for facilitators who are doing a midway evaluation for their part as discussion leaders for an ongoing Scripture study, the questions might be: "How do you think you did in the area of welcoming and initially attending to each group member weekly? How well did you move the group into the discussion time? Was the way you integrated and facilitated prayer comfortable? How have you dealt with the problem people in your small group? How do you feel about your sense of timing in moving through the discussion period? Are you able to draw your time to a comfortable closure? Are you using the feedback of your assistant regularly and fruitfully? How would you rate the support for your ministry as facilitator? Rate the facilities and set up."

c. Thank the group and ask them to sit down and share insights. Elicit via such questions/statements as: The areas of facilitating that it seems we are doing the best job at are . . . . If we had to choose the biggest problem areas they would be. . . . Facilitator could draw to a closure by saying, "My evaluation of this body voting process is. . . ." (move to the appropriate place on the continuum). Thank the group and lead them in applause.

Suggested Resource

Collaborative Ministry by Loughlan Sofield, ST and Carroll Juliano, SHCJ.

The Last Word

Your secret weapon is to choose an assistant in every group you facilitate whose main commitment is to give *YOU* regular feedback (keeps you honest with yourself).

10.

Bringing Closure to Meetings

Focus: "wrapping up," concluding each group time especially the last meeting in a series

Means: simple ways, words, prayers, rituals, celebrations

It takes skill and planning to initiate meetings in a way that helps each person feel welcomed and invited into group and into the meeting's focus. It is just as important to bring each meeting (and particularly the last meeting of a series) to a satisfying closure. This means a *wrapping up* that attends to both content and people realities (considering that the two purposes of every group are task and relationships—as outlined in Chapter 2).

The point is that without some attention to closure, every meeting ends up feeling loose-ended, unfinished, incomplete. The facilitator needs to *tie up loose ends* and affirm people growth in simple satisfying ways. This enables both leadership and group members to *let go* of that group experience and move on as part of a healthy growth process.

Below are some suggestions for concluding every meeting with attention to both task and relationship realities. Included are ways to bring closure to one time gatherings (whether short or long) as well as ideas for concluding each meeting that is part of a series (such as a regular parish staff meeting or each week of a ten week scripture study series). Most appropriately, this whole section (Chapters 5-10) that has focused on skills for facilitating will conclude with creative ways to *wrap up* the final meeting of a series.

Closure Ideas for One Time Gatherings

For short meetings such as a gathering to get parish input on the needs of the parish plant, save the last five minutes of group time to do the following.

- Facilitator either elicits from the group or gives a summary of meeting content plus any decisions made.
- Ask for the simplest form of evaluation such as "Thumbs up? Thumbs down? regarding this meeting + ONE WORD explanations (see Chapter 9 for other quick methods).
- Give a one sentence statement of gratitude for the gift of time, energy and ideas given by those present as well as a commitment to honor their input.
- State, "The meeting is over. God bless you for coming."

For a lengthy one time gathering such as an all day retreat, consider a two fold wrap-up.

- Capsulize the day's focus together via eliciting a potpourri of insights/feelings arising out of the day's experiences whether positive or negative. It is important to accept each contribution with something as simple as "Thank you" and not do problem solving. If it is a meeting that involved decision making, it is also important to add a statement summarizing any decisions made or actions agreed upon.
- Acknowledge gratitude for the gifts of the day—God present, their presence, renewal, etc. Enable a prayerful mood (stand, quiet yourself, perhaps join hands) then elicit one word articulation of any gift from the day. Add your "Amen." Send them home with, "Thanks and God bless you."

Closure Ideas for Meetings That Are Ongoing/Part of a Series

At the end of each meeting that is ongoing (such as a parish staff meeting) or a meeting that is part of a series (such as a Scripture Study).

- Summarize the yearly goals and that meeting's main agenda decisions (for a parish staff meeting) or capsulize the weekly focus of the series so far (for a Scripture study) then give a BRIEF preview of what's ahead.
- When possible, specifically acknowledge the people gifts given of presence, commitment, ideas, warmth. Finish with some form of blessing from Scripture (read or paraphrase Numbers 6:24-26 or Ephesians 3:14-21, for instance) or create your own one sentence blessing from the theme of the meeting: "May God bless you with a heart that knows justice and speaks the truth—as in the prophets. Amen."

Closure Ideas for the Final Meeting of a Season/Series

There are some very basic ingredients that need to be part of the final meeting of a series (such as a 6 week Adult Education offering in a parish) or the final meeting of the year (for the parish council, for instance).

Acknowledgements that specifically honor the workers. It is important to recognize all those who shared responsibility whether for a series or for a term of commitment. Acknowledge each by name, asking her/him to stand while you acknowledge their specific gift to the group. If their length of commitment was long, consider giving each a small token of appreciation (a flower, plant, plaque, book). Give them a special part in the closing ritual as well.

Evaluation that gives specific and helpful feedback. It is most important to do a thorough evaluation at the end of a lengthy commitment. Chapter 9 includes many creative ideas. Choose one that fits your group.

Ritual that mutually blesses participants/leadership. More than words are needed at the last meeting. It is best to use sign and symbol and involve all the participants in order to bring the best sense of a warm *wrap up*. Consider first the size of group and its focus when choosing an appropriate closure prayer/ritual. Here are a variety of ideas to use/modify/adapt.

- Give everyone a new nametag for the last meeting. Have each one write on the back one need he/she has or would like another in the group to pray for. Put all the nametags in a basket and have each draw one out. Ask everyone to put the nametag in a place where it will be a reminder to pray and remember.
- Sing a song such as "Shalom, O My Friends" while doing a significant action such as offering the Kiss of Peace to each participant. One way to do this is with two concentric circles, the inside circle facing outward and the outside circle facing inward. Have the inside circle move to the left (while the outside circle stays stationery) after each phrase, clasp the hands of the one in the opposite circle while singing/saying the words.
- Offer a reciprocal final blessing in the following manner: the ministry team stands in front with hands raised in the traditional blessing manner; Ask the group to lift their hands in the same manner as they bless the team members in return. Team says or sings the blessing (one line at a time) and has group echo back:

  > "May the blessing of God be upon you. May Christ's peace abide in you. May the Spirit illuminate your heart, Now and forevermore."

- Collect a large number of empty shells. Place them in a container. With appropriate music in the background, invite each person to walk forward and collect one shell as a reminder: Just as a hermit crab moves from shell to shell as it grows, leaving the smaller shell behind as it grows, so too, each participant has grown and the shell can be a reminder of the need to move on to further growth.

- Have a large urn of sand up front. Give everyone a taper/candle. At the end of the meeting time, play or sing appropriate music while each comes forward and lights their taper (representing their gift of themselves, their spirit light) from one large candle representing the light of Christ. Have them put their taper into the sand urn to show the power of communal light when gathered together. Plan one minute of silent prayer after all are seated.

- Ask each to bring with them to that meeting, a scripture passage or a prayer of the heart written down anonymously on a small sheet of paper. Collect them at the beginning of the meeting. At the meeting's end, while playing some appropriate music, pass the basket around and have each person take one to use.

- Try a *nurture shower* if the group is fairly small and caring. Facilitator explain the process and then lead it as follows: ask group to stand and hold hands; take a minute to quiet the inner self and be prayerfully present to one another; *shower* one group member at a time with one word or phrase affirmations as the facilitator says each name and waits for response. Another method is to place one group member at a time in the center of the circle and to write and paste on her/him post-it note words/phrases.

- Facilitator give a short and simple but personally thought out blessing for the group, one that is connected to the theme of the series: "May the knowledge of Jesus gained in this study of the gospels grow into a deeper and deeper knowing of Christ the Lord." If appropriate, ask each small group member to offer their own simple blessing for their small group as a whole. "May God bless you with . . . until we meet again."

Celebration that flows from the life of the group

- Potluck and story: tell the group to bring anything they want to share—or bring anything that is a fingerfood—

or bring any salad—or bring any dessert to go with a brown bag lunch/dinner. Have them sit with their small group and share one story/experience of grace/growth/specialness with the other small group members. Pull large group together at the end to close with a sung blessing.

- Build a sandwich and make a collage: have them bring any innards for sandwich making (condiments, lettuce, tomato, meats, cheeses, oleo, etc.) while the team members bring breads. Ask each to also bring one small piece of colored paper, cut or torn in a meaningful shape OR a small piece of material of a texture, color shape that somehow represents the person. Provide a large piece of tagboard and glue. Have each one put their contribution on with glue as they approach the food table. Facilitator guide creating a collage to symbolize the creative unity of the group. At the very end, surface words that come to mind when looking at the collage as a large group. Sing a *thanks* and an *Amen*.
- Create a salad (or create a soup) and *build an altar* (especially for a spirituality focused series). The ministry team provides the salad base, rolls and butter. Ask each participant to bring ANY salad topping or dressing (or any vegetable—cut up and ready to add to the soup stock prepared by the ministry team). In addition ask participants to bring one small stone as a symbol of their personal response to the revelation of God discovered through the series. At the end of the meeting have each person add their stone to the pile begun by the facilitator as they approach the table. At the end of the final meeting time, place a votive candle on the top, ask the group to join around the *altar*, light the candle, read a scripture, sing or say a final blessing/prayer.

Suggested Resource

Gentle, instrumental music such as the meditation tapes offered by Lura Media or Credence Cassettes.

The Last Word

Good closure brings an "AHHhh, everything's okay, it's time to go" feeling inside rather than an "UH oh, something's not quite right, what should I do next" feeling. "Hemming" our time together with conscious closure keeps all from a feeling of unraveling.

The *Last* "Last Word"

Try some of the ideas in these chapters.

Do what you can, however, not what you can't!

Start small and grow more skilled gradually.

The steps to maturity are necessarily immature!!

God bless your journeying.

Bibliography

Baronowski, Arthur *Creating Small Faith Communities*, 1989, St. Anthony Messenger Press, 1615 Republic Street, Cincinnati, Ohio 45210.

Coleman, Lyman, *Serendipity Series*, 1979, Serendipity House, Box 1012, Littleton, CO 80160.

Doohan, Helen, *The Minister of God*, 1986, Society of St. Paul, 2187 Victory Boulevard, Staten Island, NY 10314.

Ferder, Fran, *Words Made Flesh*, 1986, Ave Maria Press, Notre Dame, IN 46556.

Hays, Edward, *Pray Always*, 1981, Forest of Peace Books, Route One, Box 247, Easton, KS 66020.

Johnson, David W., and Frank P. Johnson, *Joining Together*, 1975, Prentice Hall, Englewood Cliffs, NJ 07632.

Keating, Charles, *Dealing with Difficult People*, 1984, Paulist Press, New York/Ramsey.

Meditative Music tapes by Credence Cassettes, 115 E. Armour Boulevard, P.O. Box 419492, Kansas City, MO 64141-6492, or Lura Media, P.O. Box 261668, San Diego, CA 92126.

Sofield, Loughlan, ST and Carroll Juliano SHCJ, *Collaborative Ministry,* 1987, Ave Maria Press, Notre Dame, IN 46556.